Christians and Jews Together

Series by the Messianic Jewish Theological Institute (MJTI):

Messiah and Jewish Life Series

Messiah and Judaism Series

Messiah and Jewish Vision Series

Messiah and Christians Series

Messiah and Israel Series

Christians and Jews Together

STUART DAUERMANN

WIPF & STOCK · Eugene, Oregon

CHRISTIANS AND JEWS TOGETHER

Messiah and Christians Series 1

Messianic Jewish Theological Institute
P.O. Box 54410
Los Angeles, CA 90054
www.mjti.com

Wipf & Stock
A Division of Wipf and Stock Publishers
199 W. 8th Ave., Suite 3
Eugene, OR 97401

www.wipfandstock.com

ISBN 13: 978-1-60608-403-8

Manufactured in the U.S.A.

I F YOU are an active Christian, you will not want to waste your life serving yesterday's agenda. While respecting the past, you will want to be relevant in the present out of responsibility for the future. Let me tell you about one such relevant Christian.

Picture Marcia.[1] A well-dressed, well-spoken woman in her late-sixties, single, and a member of a well-respected church in Southern California. Marcia is typical of thousands of such women. But in some ways, Marcia is very different. She elected to spend forty years of her life in a South American jungle, developing literacy materials and a Bible translation for a language spoken by only one hundred and sixty people on the face of the earth. Of that tribe, she and her translation partner had contact with only eighty people, most of whom did not understand why Marcia was bothering to do all of this. Meanwhile, back home in her comfortable church, some thought, "What a shame. Couldn't Marcia have served God back here, gotten married, and lived decently instead of in a hut without plumbing in the middle of some jungle? I suppose what she's doing is admirable, but to tell the truth, I wonder if she's wasting her life!"

I knew Marcia. We went to the same school. And she was utterly content with the life she had chosen, because she recognized her jungle existence to be her authentic response to God's call and the priorities of His Kingdom. She viewed giving this tribe the Scriptures in their own language for current and future generations to be more than worth the sacrifice she was making. But

---

1. This is a pseudonym for the sake of privacy.

make no mistake about it: there were plenty of people both in the jungle and in her church who just didn't get it.

Marcia is typical of many of God's servants who don't conform to conventional expectations. These are the kind of people whom the establishment writes off as wasting their lives, or as silly or even dangerous trouble-makers whose get up and go repeatedly gets them into tight places. It is no accident that King Ahab called the Prophet Elijah, "you troubler of Israel,"[2] and it wasn't for past-due parking tickets that Jeremiah ended up in prison, and John the Baptist lost his head. This doesn't mean, "Whenever you feel a prophetic urge, then, go for it!" After all, there are limits. But political correctness and maintaining high approval ratings aren't among them. There should be something of Elijah, Jeremiah, John and Marcia in all of us. And don't forget that irritating fellow Jesus who got himself crucified.

> *Just ask yourself, "Is the kind of Christianity I see around me forcefully advancing, and are the people in my circles doing anything worthy of attack?"*

Jesus assessed his contemporaries in words unlikely to be spoken about our generation: "From the time John the Baptist began preaching and baptizing until now, the Kingdom of Heaven has been forcefully advancing, and violent people attack it."[3] Just ask yourself, "Is the kind of Christianity I see around me forcefully advancing, and are the people in my circles doing anything worthy of attack?" If the answer is, "Not really," then read on.[4]

If we're going to work to make things better, it helps to understand the relationship between the Age to Come and the Kingdom

---

2. 1 Kgs 18:17.

3. Matt 11:12 (NLT).

4. There are some people and even some communities practicing risky, edgy, sacrificial and dynamic faith already. I know some. But my point is, these are exceptions.

of God. The Kingdom of God is a breakthrough kingdom. We encounter the Kingdom of God whenever the Age to Come (what God will finally do) invades contemporary life, demanding that we realign our today with God's tomorrow. This in-breaking is always a disruption. Think of Mary, awakened by the angel with the news she was to become the virgin mother of the Son of God. That's disruption! It was the same for Abraham and Sarah, both of them retirement age, well settled, and living in a sizable city. They sensed the call of God: "Leave your country, your people and your father's household and go to the land I will show you. I will make you into a great nation and I will bless you; I will make your name great, and you will be a blessing."[5] God's word to these seniors was "Get up and go, but I am not saying exactly where to just yet." This had risk written all over it! Fortunately, they signed on for divine inconvenience, and all of Israel, indeed all nations, are forever in their debt. The message of the Kingdom remains the same now. God is still saying, "Get up and go in the direction of what I'm doing, and I will bless you in the going."

Ask yourself the question, "Is the Age to Come disruptively breaking through in our day, or has God's Kingdom run itself down, like some spent wind-up toy?" If you don't like being bored, and if you want your life with God to count for something, these are important questions.

Give me a moment of your time, and I will show you why some of us believe aspects of the Age to Come are breaking through in our day. Then, like Abraham and Sarah, and like those twelve apostles who turned their world upside down, you will want to get with the program—to get up and go toward God's tomorrow.

More than two thousand years ago, God instructed the Prophet Habakkuk to use a template suitable to the case I am making: "Write the vision; make it plain . . . so the one may run who reads it."[6] That is the structure I will be following here: First, I will

5. Gen 12:1–2.
6. Hab 2:2.

write the vision; second, I will make it plain, situating it within the broader context of historical events and Scripture; and third, I will outline what it means to run with the vision, energized and informed by how God's Kingdom is breaking through now.

"Write the Vision"
(Habakkuk 2:2)

T HE VISION, the mandate, the new thing breaking through, is not entirely new. Hints, fragments, and pieces appear throughout the Bible. Ezekiel focuses upon it in chapters 36 and 37 of his book. While this visionary mandate centers on God's plans for the Jewish people, it has everything to do with the future of the Church and the world. Ezekiel summarizes the vision in chapter 37:21–28:

> Thus says the Lord GOD: Behold, I will take the people of Israel from the nations among which they have gone, and will gather them from all sides, and bring them to their own land; and I will make them one nation in the land, upon the mountains of Israel; and one king will be king over them all; and they will be no longer two nations, and no longer divided into two kingdoms. They will not defile themselves any more with their idols and their detestable things, or with any of their transgressions; but I will save them from all the backslidings in which they have sinned, and will cleanse them; and they will be my people, and I will be their God.
>
> My servant David will be king over them; and they will all have one shepherd. They will follow my ordinances and be careful to observe my statutes. They will dwell in the land where your fathers dwelt that I gave to my servant Jacob; they and their children and their children's children will dwell there for ever; and David my servant will be their prince for ever. I will make a covenant of peace with them; it will be an everlasting covenant with them; and I will bless them and multiply them, and will set my sanctuary in the midst of them for evermore. My dwelling place will be with them; and I will be their God, and they will be my people. Then the nations will know that I the LORD sanctify Israel, when my sanctuary is in the midst of them for evermore.

Ezekiel identifies seven aspects of God's ultimate purposes for Israel and the nations:

1   God will gather Israel from all the nations: *"Behold, I will take the people of Israel from the nations among which they have gone, and will gather them from all sides, and bring them to their own land"* (Ezek 37:21).

2   God will unify the Jewish people as one nation in the Land: *"and I will make them one nation in the land, upon the mountains of Israel; and one king will be king over them all; and they will be no longer two nations, and no longer divided into two kingdoms"* (Ezek 37:22).

3   God will spiritually renew the people of Israel: *"They will not defile themselves any more with their idols and their detestable things, or with any of their transgressions; but I will save them from all the backslidings in which they have sinned, and will cleanse them; and they will be my people, and I will be their God"* (Ezek 37:23).

4   God will gather all Israel around our Davidic King (whom we know to be Jesus the Messiah): *"My servant David will be king over them; and they will all have one shepherd"* (Ezek 37:24a).

5   God will cause all Israel to faithfully obey his Torah: *"They will follow my ordinances and be careful to observe my statutes"* (Ezek 37:24b).

6   God will bring all Israel to a full and relational experience of the Divine Presence: *"I will make a covenant of peace with them; it will be an everlasting covenant with them; and I will bless them and multiply them, and will set my sanctuary in the midst of them for evermore. My dwelling place will be with them; and I will be their God, and they will be my people"* (Ezek 37:26-27).

7   God will demonstrate to the nations once and for all that Israel is his people and that he is their God: *"Then the nations will know that I the LORD sanctify Israel, when my sanctuary is in the midst of them for evermore"* (Ezek 37:28).

"Make It Plain"
(Habakkuk 2:2)

Although Ezekiel's vision applies to all Israel, increasingly, Messianic Jews are calling it the New *Messianic* Jewish Agenda because it undergirds our vision for a new kind of Messianic Judaism.[1] For us, all aspects of this agenda are interdependent parts of God's plan for our people. For example, we are committed to covenantal Jewish life and to faith in Yeshua.[2] Neither should be neglected. This kind of Messianic Judaism is built on rediscovered scriptural foundations long buried, yet vital to God's continuing purposes for our people.

This vision may seem irrelevant to you as a Christian. It may strike you as nothing more than a quaint religious opinion unrelated to or even contradictory of Christian truth as you know it. "But wait!" as the infomercials put it. This vision becomes *very* exciting once it is seen against the wider context of what God is up to in the world, which mission theologians term the *missio dei* (the mission of God). Once its context and implications are unpacked, the New Messianic Jewish Agenda changes everything. Exploring this vision and its implications for the Church and for the Jewish people will be one of the big "Aha! moments" of your life. So let's explore it together, and "make it plain."

There is nothing timid or conventional about the Kingdom of God nor about new paradigms like this one. C. S. Lewis reminds

---

1. The Union of Messianic Jewish Congregations (UMJC) defines Messianic Judaism as "a movement of Jewish congregations and groups committed to Yeshua the Messiah that embrace the covenantal responsibility of Jewish life and identity rooted in Torah, expressed in tradition, and renewed and applied in the context of the New Covenant. Messianic Jewish groups may also include those from non-Jewish backgrounds who have a confirmed call to participate fully in the life and destiny of the Jewish people."

2. Yeshua is Jesus' original Hebrew name.

us that Aslan isn't a tame lion. South African Mission Theologian David Bosch, who exposed and resisted the evils of apartheid at the risk of his life, was no tame lion himself. He applies paradigm theories native to the field of science to the world of theology and mission, and shows how disruptive they can be:

> [A shifting of paradigms] seldom happens without a struggle, however, since scientific communities [and theological traditions] are by nature conservative and do not like their peace to be disturbed, the old paradigm's protagonists continue for a long time to fight a rearguard action. . . . Proponents of the old paradigm often just cannot understand the arguments of the proponents of the new. Metaphorically speaking, the one is playing chess and the other checkers on the same board.
>
> . . . This explains why defenders of the old order and champions of the new frequently argue at cross-purposes. Protagonists of the old paradigm, in particular, tend to immunize themselves against the arguments of the new. They resist its challenges with deep emotional reactions, since those challenges threaten to destroy their very perception and experience of reality, indeed their entire world.[3]

Remember my friend Marcia. Not everyone in her church and almost no one on her mission field understood her decisions or appreciated her sacrifice. If you are going to investigate these new ideas, even if they are God's new ideas, you too may be misunderstood. Despite this risk, I invite you to follow along as I point out a Kingdom controversy most people have yet to consider.

---

3. David Bosch, *Transforming Mission: Paradigm Shifts in Theology of Mission* (Maryknoll, NY: Orbis, 1992), 184–85. In part, Bosch's argument paraphrases Paul Hiebert, "Epistemological Foundations for Science and Theology," *Theological Students Fellowship Bulletin* (March 1985): 9 and Paul Hiebert, "The Missiological Implications of an Epistemological Shift," *Theological Students Fellowship Bulletin* (May-June 1985): 12.

HOW GREAT IS THE GREAT COMMISSION?

Consider the term, "the Great Commission." This is the name the Church attaches to Yeshua's command to "go into all the world and preach the gospel" (Mark 16:15). Few pause to consider that the Bible never refers to the Great Commission by that name. The term "great" is an evaluative term registering the Church's estimation of the commission. And certainly it is *a* great commission that has informed and spurred heroic service for nearly two thousand years. But the term is a new one. The first person to use the term "the Great Commission" was probably Dutch missionary Justinian von Welz (1621–1688). And it wasn't until the nineteenth century that the Great Commission was popularized, by missionary giant Hudson Taylor, who connected the term with Matthew 28:19–20.

> *No less an authority than the Apostle Paul gives ample evidence that there is something greater than the Great Commission.*

But it really shouldn't be called "the Great Commission," as though this is God's final word to His people. No less an authority than the Apostle Paul gives ample evidence that there is something greater than the Great Commission. How so?

THE GREATER COMMISSION

In the Letter to the Romans, chapters nine through eleven, Paul is trying to understand the purposes of God for Israel and the nations. He is troubled by what he encounters in his travels: a general Jewish disinterest, even hostility to the gospel, which contrasts markedly with widespread Gentile acceptance of it. As a loyal and committed Jew, and against the background of Scripture's glorious promises concerning the descendants of Jacob, Paul is agonizing to understand both this mysterious turning away and its implications. While some are quick to suggest that Israel's hardening proves God is finished with her—Paul knows this simply cannot be true. He comes to see that Jewish resistance to the gospel is neither universal (it is "a hardening in part")[4] nor permanent (it lasts only "until the fullness of the Gentiles has come in, and so all Israel will be saved").[5] Paul pronounces a verdict of "by no means!" over the proposition that God is through with the Jews.[6]

> *Paul pronounces a verdict of "by no means!" over the proposition that God is through with the Jews.*

In Romans 11:12, he terms this Jewish indifference to the gospel as both stumbling and loss, while anticipating a brighter future for Israel, saying: "But if their transgression means riches for the world, and their loss means riches for the Gentiles, how much greater riches will their fullness bring!" Recognizing that the partial hardening that has happened to Israel is not final, he looks forward to their eventual full inclusion, which he terms "their [Israel's] fullness." Adopting his logic to our own discussion then, *if the fullness of the Gentiles is the Great Commission, then the fullness of Israel, which Paul terms "greater riches," is rightly termed "the Greater Commission."*[7]

---

4. Rom 11:25.

5. *Loc. cit.*

6. Rom 11:1.

7. The Great Commission is given as an imperative while the Greater Commission is an inference from prophesied events. Future events are not prophesied in Scripture merely for the purpose of prediction but also as a spur to preparation—thus, the Greater Commission. As a case in point, consider 2 Pet 3:11–12, "Since all these things are thus to be dissolved, what sort of persons ought you to be in lives of holiness and godliness, waiting for and hastening the coming of the day of God."

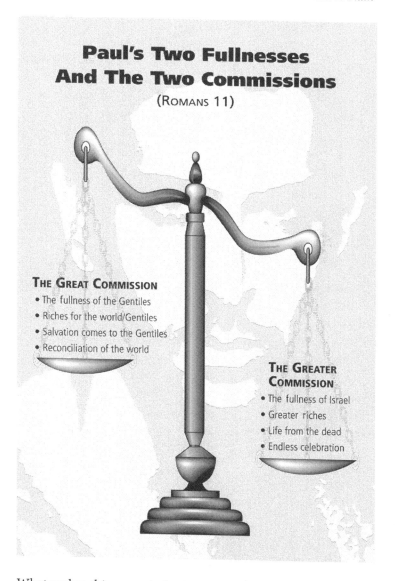

Paul's Two Fullnesses And The Two Commissions
(ROMANS 11)

THE GREAT COMMISSION
• The fullness of the Gentiles
• Riches for the world/Gentiles
• Salvation comes to the Gentiles
• Reconciliation of the world

THE GREATER COMMISSION
• The fullness of Israel
• Greater riches
• Life from the dead
• Endless celebration

What makes this commission greater is that it brings greater results. Paul says that while the trespass and stumbling of Israel resulted in the reconciliation of the world (the fullness of the nations), the fullness of Israel will mean even greater riches, life from the dead—the resurrection of all the departed, and a never-ending celebration for the entire cosmos![8]

> In Romans 11, Paul makes clear that God's consummating purpose for the Jewish people is not simply an extension of the Great Commission, but is a distinct yet related work. It is another fullness that God is pursuing.

Paul calls these astonishing outworkings of God's purpose "a mystery."[9] But what was a mystery for him is revolutionary for us, because it challenges the Church to consider how God's missional intent toward Israel and the nations is a differentiated one. In Romans 11, Paul makes clear that God's consummating purpose for the Jewish people is not simply an extension of the

Great Commission, but is a distinct yet related work. It is another fullness that God is pursuing.

The outcome of this work in the Jewish context will look very different from what God is doing among the nations, even though it is through the same Messiah Yeshua. Such thinking is contrary to long-held assumptions, but Romans 11 is clear: God's mission, what he is up to in the world, culminates in two fullnesses, not one. The New Messianic Jewish Agenda outlines the context and contours of that fullness toward which God is moving his people Israel.

---

8. Rom 11:12. Notice that Paul preserves an alternating rhythm between Israel and the nations. This is part of what theologian R. Kendall Soulen calls the theological grammar of the Bible, that humankind is never thought of as an undifferentiated whole, but always as Israel and the nations. (R. Kendall Soulen, "The Grammar of the Christian Story," *The Institute* 10 (Autumn 2000). Cited 8 August 2008. Online: http://www.icjs.org/news/vol10/soulenrevised.html). This is not because Israel is better than other people groups, but because they are "beloved for the sake of the fathers" (Rom 11:29). This two-fold division of humanity is fundamental to the biblical worldview. The language of Scripture is stark on this matter, as in Num 23:9, Deut 32:8, and Amos 3:2.

9. Rom 11:25.

But before proceeding, we must respond to the objection, "Yes, but isn't this all for later? Why do I have to deal with it now?" We must deal with it now because "later" is knocking on our door. The Age to Come is breaking in. Say "hello" to the Kingdom of God.

God is calling us to get up and go in some new directions, as the Greater Commission moves toward the center stage of world history. There are five reasons why I believe this shift is happening now.

Reason 1: The Rebirth of Israel (1948)

The Bible says history is moving toward a military crisis in the Middle East when all the nations of the world will be gathered against Jerusalem. Zechariah tells us that the Jewish people will be in the Land. Scripture says:

> I will make Jerusalem a cup of reeling to all the peoples round about.... On that day I will make Jerusalem a heavy stone for all the peoples; all who lift it will grievously hurt themselves. And all the nations of the earth will come together against it (Zech 12:2–3).[10]

This and other prophetic texts tell us that the Jewish people must be in the Land of Israel at the end of days. After two thousand years, the necessary preconditions for these events came into place with the birth of the modern Jewish State in 1948. The rebirth of Israel in our days is a sign that we are living in a time of preparation for the consummation of all things, involving the Greater Commission and the New Messianic Jewish Agenda.

---

10. See also Zech 12:9; Deut 30:1–5; Jer 30:10–11, 18–24; 50:33–34; Ezek 36:6–24; Joel 3:19–21; Obad 15–21.

Reason 2: The Liberation of Jerusalem (1967)

The same text in Zechariah reminds us not only that the Jewish people are going to be dwelling in the Land, but that Jerusalem is going to be a Jewish city. This became a reality after two thousand years with the Six Day War in 1967. This too is a sign of the times, and a sign that preconditions for fulfillment are taking place.

Reason 3: The Regathering of Jews to Israel, Especially From the North

Scripture reminds us that part of the nexus of events concerning Israel in the latter days is the regathering of Jewish exiles not only from the nations in general, but explicitly "from the land of the north," a term commonly associated with the Former Soviet Union (FSU), located north of Israel. Many are old enough to remember when it was front page news when one Jew from the Former Soviet Union made it to Israel. It was in this context that the term *refusenik* entered common parlance, referring to Jews whom the Soviet Union refused permission to emigrate to Israel. But during the days of *glasnost* and *perestroika* under Mikhail Gorbachev, and especially after the break-up of the FSU, all of this changed dramatically.

What a contrast between the early 1980s and today. In the intervening years, over one million Jews have emigrated from the Former Soviet Union to Israel, so that today one in five Israeli Jews is from the FSU! When we combine this information with other Jewish immigration statistics, like the massive airlifts of Ethiopian Jews, of whom over 85,000 have emigrated to Israel in the same time frame, we grasp the accuracy and relevance of this passage penned some 2,600 years ago by the Prophet Jeremiah:

> So then, the days are coming when they will say, "As surely as the LORD lives, who brought the descendants of Israel up out of the land of the north and out of all the countries

where he had banished them." Then they will live in their own land (Jer 23:8–9).

This too is a compelling reason for saying that the Great Director is setting up the final scene of history.

Reason 4: Spiritual Renewal of the Jewish People

Deuteronomy 30 and Ezekiel 36, among other passages,[11] connect the return of the Jewish people to the Land with a return to covenant faithfulness—to obeying God's statutes and ordinances, in spiritually-renewed heartfelt devotion. This too is happening, at least in preliminary stages. The Shoah destroyed most of the centers of religious Judaism, and, as with other religious communities, secularism has left its mark on the children of Israel. And yet, Judaism maintains its vitality today. Jewish religious observance is on the rise, and many formerly secularized Jews are returning to the ways of their ancestors. Even the Reform movement is experiencing a formerly unimaginable return to Jewish ritual life among those representing what is now termed "Observant Reform." In the Land of Israel, spiritual renewal is evident among groups of secular Jews, who on their own initiative are studying sacred texts.[12]

Jewish Yeshua-faith is also on the rise. Large numbers of Jewish people began coming to faith in Yeshua the Messiah about the same time as the liberation of Jerusalem in 1967. Despite ebbs and flows, this upsurge continues. Many of those Jews who have come to Israel from "the land of the north," the Former Soviet Union, are Yeshua-believing Jews. Today, every Israeli congregation of Jewish Yeshua-believers includes a substantial number of Russian speakers. Knowledgeable observers concur that Yeshua-faith is on the rise among Israeli Jews. A recent report states:

11. Cf. Deut 30:6; Ezek 36:27; 37:24b, 26.

12. Based on a private conversation with Dr. Tsvi Sadan, an Israeli expert on contemporary Israeli attitudes toward Yeshua, July 2008.

> Although nobody knows for sure how many Messianic Jews
> live in Israel, it's believed there are about 120 congregations
> now and 10,000-15,000 Jewish believers in Jesus. That may
> not sound like many given Israel's nearly six million Jews,
> but it's a far cry from 10 years ago when there were only
> about 3,500 Jewish believers and 80 congregations.[13]

The Spirit of God seems to be doing a new thing. Dry bones are stirring and coming together in Israel and around the world.[14]

Reason 5: Renewal of a Concern for Messianic Jewish Covenant Faithfulness

As one involved in the modern Messianic Jewish movement since the early 1960s, I can confidently say that at that time the idea of Jews living according to Torah as a matter of obedience was almost entirely absent. It was not so much rejected as ignored—a non-issue that rarely came up. Most of us had imbibed the theological assumption that Jewish covenantal living was not necessary for Messianic Jews. In recent years, many of us, not only in the United States, but also in Israel, Europe, and around the world, are having a "Why didn't we ever see this before?" experience with the scriptural imperative to honor the God of our ancestors in the context of Jewish covenantal life. We now see ourselves not only in covenant with God, but also with our people Israel.

In the early decades after the founding of the modern State of Israel, Yeshua believers conformed to the culture of the missionary, a problem similar to that experienced in western mission activity in Africa and Asia. In the current renewal, many Jewish Yeshua believers are conforming to Torah and to Jewish covenantal living.

13. Wendy Griffith, "Israel's Messianic Jews: Some Call it a Miracle," n.p. [cited 1 September 2008]. Online: http://www.cbn.com/CBNnews/407139.aspx.

14. See Ezek 37:1–14.

Maybe your Christian experience has taught you to think of this kind of talk as irrelevant because, after all, the Church is the New Israel. This widely held position is called "replacement theology" or "supersessionism." William Vlach defines supersessionism as a view based on two core beliefs:

> (1) national Israel has somehow completed or forfeited its status as the people of God and will never again possess a unique role or function apart from the church; and (2) the church is now the true Israel that has permanently replaced or superseded national Israel as the people of God. Supersessionism, then, in the context of Israel and the church, is the view that *the New Testament church is the new Israel that has forever superseded national Israel as the people of God.* The result is that the church has become the sole inheritor of God's covenant blessings originally promised to national Israel in the Old Testament.[15]

While this cluster of assumptions still lingers in many Christian minds, theologies, and institutions, supersessionism is being increasingly abandoned by many as a vestige of a sad and ancient legacy of Christian anti-Judaism and anti-Semitism. The Shoah (the Holocaust) and the founding of the modern Jewish State triggered this reconsideration and rejection of replacement theology. The Shoah demonstrated that Christian assumptions about the Church being spiritually superior to the Jewish people were groundless. Recognizing its own passivity and complicity during the Shoah, and its responsibility for perpetuating contempt of the Jewish people and their religion, many church bodies are turning from their elitism and revising their theological statements. The founding of the modern State of Israel, rising phoenix-like from crematoria ash, has demonstrated that God is far from through with

15. Michael J. Vlach, "Defining Supersessionism," n.p. [cited 8 December 2008]. Online: http://www.theologicalstudies.citymax.com/articles/article/1546-226/17515.htm.

the Jews. Since God is not through with "the old Israel," it makes little sense to imagine he has replaced it with a new Israel![16]

But what are we to do with all of this? Amidst this shifting theological landscape, can we identify stable and appropriate pathways of faithfulness? Yes, we can. And toward that end, we come to the third major division of our discussion.

16. Some terms used of the people of Israel in the Older Testament are extended to apply to the Church in the Newer Testament, as in 1 Peter 2, where the Church is termed a royal priesthood and a holy nation, terms originally found in Exodus 19. It is one thing to *extend* a term to apply it to a new body of people and quite another to *transfer* that term from one body to another.

Running with the Vision

"Write the vision, make it plain . . . so the one may run who reads it."

(Habakkuk 2:2)

TURNING NOW to explore the practical implications of what we have been saying so far, how can we run with this vision? Answering this question involves answering three subsidiary questions: Who are the servants of the *Greater* Commission? Who are the servants of the *Great* Commission? What should be the Church's relationship to the Greater Commission? Let's deal with each in turn.

WHO ARE THE SERVANTS OF THE GREATER COMMISSION?

The Messianic Jewish Remnant are the primary servants of the Greater Commission. The Messianic Jewish Remnant are those Jews who believe in Yeshua and who seek to live among their own people, endeavoring to live Jewish lives of covenantal obedience. But what is this Remnant supposed to do as servants of the Greater Commission?

God calls the Messianic Jewish Remnant to serve the Greater Commission by being a sign, demonstration, and catalyst foreshadowing Israel's final destiny. This Remnant must embody the New Messianic Jewish Agenda. Don't imagine that this is some sort of trendy bumper-sticker concept, easily and wisely avoided. Instead, it is an update of the kind of intentionality shown by Jesus and the Apostles, but for a new day and context. Mission theologian Stan Nussbaum reminds us that Jesus, the Apostles, and the early church were themselves signs, demonstrations and catalysts of the Kingdom:

Jesus and the early church understood that it was not their mission to impose the revolution of God's reign but only to signal it. They did not overthrow Rome; they only acted as if they knew of something or someone more powerful and important than Rome. They did not pressure Rome to legislate equality between citizens and non-citizens; they showed the world what such equality looked like. They were gentle signs of things to come.[1]

The Messianic Jewish Remnant, servants of the Greater Commission, must become in our day and context what Yeshua and the Apostles were in their own: a sign, demonstration and catalyst of God's good things to come. Like them, we don't force the future, but rather invite it in, allowing it to shape us, while we energetically prepare for the fullness of Israel.

WHO ARE THE SERVANTS OF THE GREAT COMMISSION?

You probably already know the answer to this question. The primary servants of the Great Commission are Christians, that body of believers from among the nations, called to gather the fullness of the nations, thus hastening the consummation of all things. Although the Great Commission is certainly not the sum total of Christian responsibility, it is a major component of the Christian's job description, to "Go therefore and make disciples of all nations, baptizing them in the name of the Father and of the Son and of the Holy Spirit, teaching them to observe all that I have commanded you; and lo, I am with you always, to the close of the age."[2] Christians help to hasten the close of the present age and to hasten the Age to Come by neither forgetting nor neglecting their job description.

1. David Nussbaum, *A Reader's Guide to "Transforming Mission"* (Maryknoll, NY: Orbis, 2005), 20.

2. Matt 28:19–20.

Together, the Messianic Jewish Remnant, living in the context of Jewish community and covenant faithfulness, and Christians from among the nations, constitute what Paul calls "One New Man." But this One New Man is created not through abolishing differences, but rather by overcoming them, bringing unity (not uniformity) between two communities that remain essentially distinct. Although many translations have trouble expressing this nuance, the Weymouth New Testament gets it right:

> *Together, the Messianic Jewish Remnant, living in the context of Jewish community and covenant faithfulness, and Christians from among the nations, constitute what Paul calls "One New Man."*

> His design was to unite the two sections of humanity in Himself so as to form one new man, thus effecting peace, and to reconcile Jews and Gentiles in one body to God, by means of His cross—slaying by it their mutual enmity. So He came and proclaimed good news of peace to you who were so far away, and peace to those who were near; because it is through Him that Jews and Gentiles alike have access through one Spirit to the Father.[3]

Paul continues to preserve this tension between unity and diversity, the differentiated unity of the One New Man, when he says later, "This mystery is that through the gospel the Gentiles are heirs together with Israel, members together of one body, and sharers together in the promise in Christ Jesus."[4] The threefold repetition of the term "together," reflects the details of the Greek text, and emphasizes that the One New Man is comprised of two

3. Eph 2:15b–18 (Weymouth). Paul indicates that this reconciliation between the Messianic Jewish Remnant and Gentile Christians has profound implications for the rest of the Jewish world as well, saying that what happens to the root effects the branches, and what happens to the lump effects the status of the entire harvest (Rom 11:16).

4. Eph 3:6 (NIV).

communities that continue to walk together in that differentiated unity God has created through Yeshua the Messiah.

WHAT SHOULD BE THE CHURCH'S RELATIONSHIP TO THE GREATER COMMISSION?

We can clarify this relationship by considering the meaning of the term "paramission." Paramission ("alongside mission") highlights the responsibility of Christians from among the nations and the Messianic Jewish Remnant to come alongside and help one another. Therefore, the paramission of the Messianic Jewish Remnant is to assist Christians in their service to the Great Commission (the fullness of the nations). Likewise, the paramission of Christians is to assist the Messianic Jewish Remnant in their service to the Greater Commission (the fullness of Israel).

Why should Christians concern themselves with assisting the Messianic Jewish Remnant in accomplishing the Greater Commission?

Why should Christians concern themselves with assisting the Messianic Jewish Remnant in accomplishing the Greater Commission? This may be compared to being invited to a great feast at which Jews are not admitted without bringing Gentile friends, nor Gentiles admitted without bringing Jewish friends. According to Paul, the Great Commission must run its course in gathering the fullness of the nations, and the Greater Commission must run its course in gathering the fullness of Israel. After the fullness of Israel and the fullness of the nations have been gathered, God will convene a celebration for the entire cosmos, beginning with the resurrection of the dead. Both Commissions, leading to the consummation of God's purposes for Israel and the nations, must be fulfilled. We might term Christians committed to this perspective "Two Commission Christians."

TWO COMMISSION CHRISTIANS AND THE NEW MESSIANIC JEWISH AGENDA

Two Commission Christians are those who recognize and advance what Scripture teaches, that God is gathering two fullnesses, the fullness of the nations and the fullness of Israel. Although their primary mission is the Great Commission, the paramission of Two Commission Christians is to help the Messianic Jewish Remnant to accomplish what God is doing among the Jewish people, what we have been calling the New Messianic Jewish Agenda. How might they practically assist the Messianic Jewish Remnant in this way? Consider, for example, these recommended responses following each item of the New Messianic Jewish Agenda:

1. God will gather Israel from all the nations: "Behold, I will take the people of Israel from the nations among which they have gone, and will gather them from all sides, and bring them to their own land" (Ezek 37:21).

   - *Christian Response*: Two Commission Christians support the Jewish return to the Land of our ancestors and the establishment of a stable Jewish state within secure borders.[5]

2. God will unify the Jewish people as one nation in the Land: "[A]nd I will make them one nation in the land, upon the mountains of Israel; and one king will be king over them all; and they will be no longer two nations, and no longer divided into two kingdoms" (Ezek 37:22).

---

5. This is not to suggest that Two Commission Christians should support every decision of the Israeli government. Israel makes mistakes. Having reservations about governmental policies and practices, however, should not prevent Two Commission Christians from affirming the God-given mandate and right of Jews to return to the Land of Promise, and to live there in peace, within secure borders.

- *Christian Response*: Two Commission Christians see the Jewish people as one people, and will support Messianic Jews in honoring their Jewish identity and communal responsibilities.

- *Christian Response*: Two Commission Christians see the assimilation of Jews into other contexts as a negative.

3. God will spiritually renew the people of Israel: "They will not defile themselves any more with their idols and their detestable things, or with any of their transgressions; but I will save them from all the backslidings in which they have sinned, and will cleanse them; and they will be my people, and I will be their God" (Ezek 37:23).

   - *Christian Response*: Two Commission Christians pray for, assist, and welcome all signs of the Jewish people being renewed in their love of God and loyalty to him.

4. God will gather all Israel around our Davidic King (whom we know to be Yeshua the Messiah): "My servant David will be king over them; and they will all have one shepherd" (Ezek 37:24a).

   - *Christian Response*: Two Commission Christians encourage Jewish faith in Yeshua.

   - *Christian Response*: Two Commission Christians encourage the Messianic Jewish Remnant as it interprets Yeshua to the Jewish world.

5. God will cause all Israel to faithfully obey his Torah: "They will follow my ordinances and be careful to observe my statutes" (Ezek 37:24b).

   - *Christian Response*: Two Commission Christians support Jewish efforts toward Torah living. In agreement with the rest of Scripture, the Apostle Paul taught that Gentile Yeshua believers are not obligated to keep Torah. Yet Paul so lived and taught as to affirm that all Jews, including Messianic Jews, *are* called to Torah living in their service to God.

6. God will bring all Israel to a full and relational experience of the Divine Presence: "I will make a covenant of peace with them; it will be an everlasting covenant with them; and I will bless them and multiply them, and will set my sanctuary in the midst of them for evermore. My dwelling place will be with them; and I will be their God, and they will be my people" (Ezek 37:26–27).

   - *Christian Response*: Two Commission Christians pray for and assist the Messianic Jewish Remnant as it seeks and practices the reality of the Divine Presence in the midst of the people of Israel, while not expecting that this Presence be manifest in ways the Church has come to expect.

7. God will demonstrate to the nations once and for all that Israel is his people and that he is their God: "Then the nations will know that I the LORD sanctify Israel, when my sanctuary is in the midst of them for evermore" (Ezek 37:28).

   - *Christian Response*: Two Commission Christians defend the honor of Yeshua and the chosenness of Israel, in the face of popular rejection of both. Yeshua and the Jewish people remain bones of contention in the world. As part of his consummating purpose, God will vindicate Yeshua and Israel in the sight of all, indicating that Yeshua is his beloved Son and Israel his beloved people.

In brief then, Two Commission Christians support and serve this agenda as their paramission, advancing the consummation we all long and strive for. This is not just a nice idea or one option among many, but rather an urgent call to assist in matters pivotal to the consummation of all things. It is all the more urgent because Two Commission Christians are presently a minority, while most of the

Church, schooled in replacement theology, ignores or is unaware of what God is doing in the Greater Commission.

Let's summarize then how Two Commission Christians live out the implications of this new paradigm:

In *attitude*, Two Commission Christians are alert to anti-Jewish assumptions both within themselves and in their contexts. God is not through with the Jewish people, and the well-being of the Church and of the cosmos depends upon the progress and fulfillment of the Greater Commission. Being a Two Commission Christian entails embracing and advancing concerns widely rejected by the Church, that Jews ought to live in the land of Israel, and that Messianic Jews ought to honor their covenant with God through faithfulness to Torah. This contradicts centuries of Christian theologizing which has long advocated one path of obedience for Jew and Gentile alike (a law-free gospel), wrongly asserting an undifferentiated nature of the One New Man.

Two Commission Christians investigate, develop, and embrace a post-supersessionist theology. They reexamine and, in some cases, replace old constructs.

In *action*, Two Commission Christians remember and serve their primary commission, the Great Commission, while supporting the Jewish community whenever aspects of the New Messianic Jewish Agenda (the unfolding of the Greater Commission) are being advanced. The Great Commission and the Greater Commission, while distinct, are interdependent, so that neither Christians nor Messianic Jews can afford to be apathetic about the progress each community is making. It is only as both commissions advance that the consummation draws near.

In the area of evangelism, called "outreach" in Jewish circles, Two Commission Christians realize how inappropriate it is to bring Jews to faith in Christ apart from honoring the other aspects of the New Messianic Jewish Agenda. Bringing Jews to Christ without bringing them near to Torah and to the Jewish community continues the legacy of replacement theology which Two Commission Christians have left behind.

Two Commission Christians actively support the Messianic Jewish Remnant as it serves the New Messianic Jewish Agenda. For example, the Messianic Jewish Theological Institute (MJTI), with the mission statement "Teaching and living a vision of Jewish life renewed in Yeshua," serves the New Messianic Jewish Agenda. We advance the Greater Commission, especially through proclaiming Yeshua as the one through whom the New Messianic Jewish Agenda reaches fulfillment. We invite and need the support of Christians in praying, giving, and advocacy, hoping they will in turn win others to our perspective and endeavor.

> *Bringing Jews to Christ without bringing them near to Torah and to the Jewish community continues the legacy of replacement theology which Two Commission Christians have left behind.*

In forming *alliances*, Two Commission Christians seek out ways for their churches and related Christian institutions to partner with the wider Jewish world in matters of common concern.

Some Christian agencies concern themselves with bringing the good news of Yeshua to Jewish people. However, I know of no mission agency that follows the Two Commission model, treating Jewish covenant faithfulness as a God-given priority for all Jews, and Jewish return to the Land as a divine imperative. If the Two Commissions model is valid, the Church and the Messianic Jewish Remnant must create agencies that coordinate Great Commission and Greater Commission programs to expedite the consummation of all things.[6]

In the area of *awareness*, Two Commission Christians recognize that not everyone is happy with this point of view. Many,

6. I especially recommend Messianic Jewish Theological Institute (www.mjti .org), the Messianic Jewish Rabbinical Council (www.ourrabbis.com) and other such organizations which are committed to the New Messianic Jewish Agenda and have developed within the Union of Messianic Jewish Congregations (www .umjc.org).

well-meaning and sincere, instinctively believe that preserving the status quo is categorically better than new initiatives of any kind. Remember my friend Marcia, and how many in her church were unsettled by her unusual choices. Some will greet this new perspective with distrust and even disdain. Others may be entrenched in theological systems which do not recognize the Two Commissions paradigm, and oppose it on supersessionist bases. Two Commission Christians should not simply react, nor attempt to force the issue, realizing that getting used to new ideas takes time. In many cases, the best one can hope for is that differing parties will agree to disagree.

FINAL THOUGHTS

There Are Always Winners and Losers
When the Paradigm Changes

Joel Barker is an independent scholar and futurist who popularized the term "paradigm shift" in his book, *Paradigms: The Business of Discovering the Future.*[7] He tells a true story about the Swiss watchmaking industry. It is a story we cannot afford to miss.

In 1968, the Swiss sold sixty-five percent of the watches manufactured worldwide and controlled well over eighty percent of watchmaking profits. They dominated watchmaking by making the best mainsprings, gears, jewels, and cases. For generations it was axiomatic that if you wanted a fine watch, you wanted a Swiss watch. But by 1980, their market share collapsed to less than ten percent, and within two years, 50,000 of the 62,000 Swiss watchmakers lost their jobs. What happened?

What happened was that the Swiss slept through a paradigm shift—and when they woke up, the world had changed, while they hadn't. Almost overnight, they became irrelevant. The wave of the future—the quartz crystal watch—had become the rage. The Swiss

7. Joel Arthur Barker, *Paradigms: The Business of Discovering the Future* (New York: HarperCollins, 1993), 15–18.

were unprepared. The wave became a tsunami decimating their share in an industry they had dominated for generations.

The Swiss should have known better! It was their scientists who invented the electronic quartz movement in 1967 at their Research Institute in Neuchâtel, Switzerland. However, the Swiss manufacturers dismissed the idea. "Everyone knows that watches are made with gears and springs! You call yourselves scientists and you don't know that?" They didn't like this non-conformist idea. They showed the scientists the door, and took them off the A-list.

However, the Swiss industrial magnates thought the idea was at least a cute novelty. That is why they displayed the technology as a gimmick that year at the World Watch Congress. Some Japanese observers walked by, and having the imagination and flexibility the Swiss lacked, picked up the idea and ran with it, running away with the watchmaking market as well. Meanwhile, the Swiss industry was left with a mountain of watches nobody wanted.

We are entering a climactic chapter of history. The Age to Come is breaking through, and the Kingdom of God is knocking at the door. God is turning the wheels of time and moving the Greater Commission toward the center stage of world history. Are you going to sleep through the paradigm shift like the Swiss did? Or will you join us in changing the world?

Glossary

Great Commission—The Church's name for Yeshua's parting mandate to the Apostles, "Go therefore and make disciples of all nations, baptizing them in the name of the Father and of the Son and of the Holy Spirit, and teaching them to obey everything that I have commanded you. And remember, I am with you always, to the end of the age" (Matt 28:19–20). In Pauline terms, this is Yeshua's command to gather in "the fullness of the nations," and to teach them what Messiah passed on to the Apostles. Although this command was given explicitly to the Apostles, it has been historically understood to apply to the Church throughout time. The term "Great Commission" was first used in the seventeenth century to refer to Yeshua's mandate.

Greater Commission—The mandate to gather in the fullness of Israel. Paul compares the fullness of Israel to the fullness of the nations by calling the former "greater riches" than the latter. The imperative to expedite this "greater riches" is therefore the Greater Commission.

Messianic Jewish Remnant—Those descendants of Abraham, Isaac, and Jacob who name Yeshua of Nazareth as Messiah and Lord, and who seek to honor their covenantal responsibilities toward God and each other.[1]

Missio Dei—Simply put, "What God is up to in the world."

Mission—The work that God sends his people forth to do, in conjunction with what he is up to in the world.

---

1. The Older Testament indicates that Jacob's descendants are called to a unique way of life, based on Torah, the national constitution of the Jewish people. The Newer Testament specifies that this way of life is not incumbent upon Gentile Christians (Acts 15; 21:17–26; 1 Cor 7:17–24).

New Messianic Jewish Agenda—Seven agenda items concerning the destiny of the Jewish people that ought to be embodied, served, and welcomed by the Messianic Jewish Remnant as assisted by Christians from among the nations. These agenda items are widely attested in Scripture and summarized in Ezekiel 37:21–28.

Paramission—The responsibility of Christians from among the nations and the Messianic Jewish Remnant to come alongside each other to render assistance in their respective missions.

Servants of the Great Commission—Those called to partner with God in fulfilling the Great Commission—Christians from among the nations.

Servants of the Greater Commission—Those called to partner with God in fulfilling the Greater Commission—the Messianic Jewish Remnant.

Supersessionism—Also known as "replacement theology." The view that *"the New Testament church is the new Israel that has forever superseded national Israel as the people of God. The result is that the church has become the sole inheritor of God's covenant blessings originally promised to national Israel in the Old Testament."*[2]

Two Commission Christians—Christians who pray, work, and give toward the progress of two fullnesses (of the nations and of Israel) and thus two commissions (the Great Commission and the Greater Commission).

2. Vlach, *loc. cit.*

Biblical Support for the
New Messianic Jewish Agenda

I. THE JEWISH PEOPLE IN THEIR OWN LAND
(Ezek 37:21, 25)

Isa 11:12—"He will raise an ensign for the nations, and will assemble the outcasts of Israel, and gather the dispersed of Judah from the four corners of the earth."

Isa 27:12—"and you will be gathered one by one, O people of Israel."

Isa 43:5–6—"I will bring your offspring from the east, and from the west I will gather you; I will say to the north, Give up, and to the south, Do not withhold; bring my sons from afar and my daughters from the end of the earth"

Jer 16:15—"For I will bring them back to their own land which I gave to their fathers."

Jer 29:14—"I will restore your fortunes and gather you from all the nations and all the places where I have driven you, says the LORD, and I will bring you back to the place from which I sent you into exile."

Jer 30:3—"I will bring them back to the land which I gave to their fathers, and they will take possession of it."

Jer 31:8—"Behold, I will bring them from the north country, and gather them from the farthest parts of the earth, among them the blind and the lame, the woman with child and her who is in travail, together; a great company, they will return here."

Jer 31:10—"He who scattered Israel will gather him, and will keep him as a shepherd keeps his flock."

Jer 32:37—"Behold, I will gather them from all the countries to which I drove them in my anger and my wrath and in great indignation; I will bring them back to this place, and I will make them dwell in safety."

Ezek 11:17—"Thus says the Lord GOD: I will gather you from the peoples, and assemble you out of the countries where you have been scattered, and I will give you the land of Israel."

Ezek 34:13—"their own land"

Ezek 36:24—"your own land"

Amos 9:15—"I will plant them upon their land, and they will never again be plucked up out of the land which I have given them"

II. AS ONE PEOPLE
(Ezek 37:22)

Jer 3:18—"In those days the house of Judah will join the house of Israel, and together they will come from the land of the north to the land that I gave your fathers for a heritage."

Jer 50:4—"In those days and in that time, says the LORD, the people of Israel and the people of Judah will come together, weeping as they come; and they will seek the LORD their God."

Hos 1:11—"And the people of Judah and the people of Israel will be gathered together"

III. SPIRITUALLY RENEWED
(Ezek 37:23)

Ezek 11:18–19—"And when they come there, they will remove from it all its detestable things and all its abominations. And I will give them one heart, and put a new spirit within them; I will take the stony heart out of their flesh and give them a heart of flesh"

Ezek 36:25–27—"I will sprinkle clean water upon you, and you will be clean from all your uncleannesses, and from all your idols I will cleanse you."

Jer 50:20—"In those days and in that time, says the LORD, iniquity will be sought in Israel, and there will be none; and sin in Judah, and none will be found"

Ezek 20:43—"And there you will remember your ways and all the doings with which you have polluted yourselves; and you will loathe yourselves for all the evils that you have committed."

IV. AROUND THE MESSIAH
(Ezek 37:24a, 25)

Jer 23:5–6—"Behold, the days are coming, says the LORD, when I will raise up for David a righteous Branch, and he will reign as king and deal wisely, and will execute justice and righteousness in the land. In his days Judah will be saved, and Israel will dwell securely. And this is the name by which he will be called: 'The LORD is our righteousness.'"

Jer 30:9—"But they will serve the LORD their God and David their king, whom I will raise up for them."

Hos 3:4–5—"For the children of Israel will dwell many days without king or prince, without sacrifice or pillar, without ephod or teraphim. Afterward the children of Israel will return and seek the LORD their God, and David their king"

Luke 1:32—"He will be great, and will be called the Son of the Most High; and the Lord God will give to him the throne of his father David."

V. WALKING IN COVENANT FAITHFULNESS
(Ezek 37:24b, 26)

Deut 30:6—"And the LORD your God will circumcise your heart and the heart of your offspring, so that you will love the LORD your God with all your heart and with all your soul, that you may live."

Jer 31:33—"I will put my law within them, and I will write it upon their hearts"

Jer 32:39—"I will give them one heart and one way, that they may fear me for ever, for their own good and the good of their children after them."

Ezek 11:19-20—"And I will give them one heart, and put a new spirit within them; I will take the stony heart out of their flesh and give them a heart of flesh, that they may walk in my statutes and keep my ordinances and obey them."

Ezek 36:27—"And I will put my spirit within you, and cause you to walk in my statutes and be careful to observe my ordinances."

VI. WITH GOD IN THE MIDST
(Ezek 37:27, 28)

Jer 31:33—"But this is the covenant which I will make with the house of Israel after those days, says the LORD: I will put my law within them, and I will write it upon their hearts; and I will be their God, and they will be my people."

Jer 32:38—"And they will be my people, and I will be their God."

Ezek 11:20—"and they will be my people, and I will be their God."

Ezek 37:23—"I will save them from all the backslidings in which they have sinned, and will cleanse them; and they will be my people, and I will be their God."

Zech 8:8—"and I will bring them to dwell in the midst of Jerusalem; and they will be my people and I will be their God, in faithfulness and in righteousness."

Heb 8:10—"This is the covenant that I will make with the house of Israel after those days, says the Lord: I will put my laws into their minds, and write them on their hearts, and I will be their God, and they will be my people."

VII. VINDICATED IN THE SIGHT OF THE NATIONS (Ezek 37:28)

Ezek 36:23—"I will vindicate the holiness of my great name, which has been profaned among the nations, and which you have profaned among them; and the nations will know that I am the LORD, says the Lord GOD, when through you I vindicate my holiness before their eyes."

Ezek 36:36—"Then the nations that are left round about you will know that I, the LORD, have rebuilt the ruined places, and replanted that which was desolate; I, the LORD, have spoken, and I will do it."

Ezek 38:23—"So I will show my greatness and my holiness and make myself known in the eyes of many nations. Then they will know that I am the LORD."

Ezek 39:7—"And my holy name I will make known in the midst of my people Israel; and I will not let my holy name be profaned any more; and the nations will know that I am the LORD, the Holy One in Israel."

Made in the USA
Lexington, KY
01 May 2014